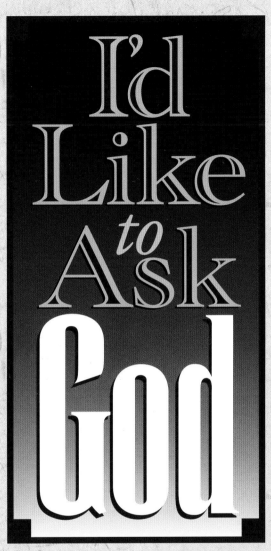

I'd Like to Ask God

Nancy Spiegelberg
Illustrated by Jane E. Ray

HARVEST
HOUSE
PUBLISHERS

Eugene, Oregon 97402

FOR RACHEL, AVERY, AND SETH
. . . AND ALL GRANDCHILDREN EVERYWHERE

Scripture quotations in this book are taken from the Holy Bible, New International Version®, Copyright © 1973, 1978, 1984 by the International Bible Society. Used by permission of Zondervan Publishing House. The "NIV" and "New International Version" trademarks are registered in the United States Patent and Trademark Office by International Bible Society.

I'D LIKE TO ASK GOD

Copyright © 1995 by Nancy Spiegelberg
Illustration © 1995 by Jane E. Ray
Published by Harvest House Publishers
Eugene, Oregon 97402

Library of Congress Cataloging-in-Publication Data
Spiegelberg, Nancy.
        I'd like to ask God / Nancy Spiegelberg: illustrated by Jane E. Ray.
        p.   cm.
        ISBN 1-56507-183-2
        1. Bible—Juvenile literature.   I. Title.
BS539.S65 1995
220.9'505—dc20   95– 13307
                                                                        CIP
                                                                        AC

Printed in Mexico.
95 96 97 98 99 00 01 — 10 9 8 7 6 5 4 3 2 1

I'd Like to Ask God

first of all,
to bless all readers
great and small.
Help us to take
a closer look
and may this
sometimes funny book
open eyes
and help us grow,
to learn from
lives
lived long ago.

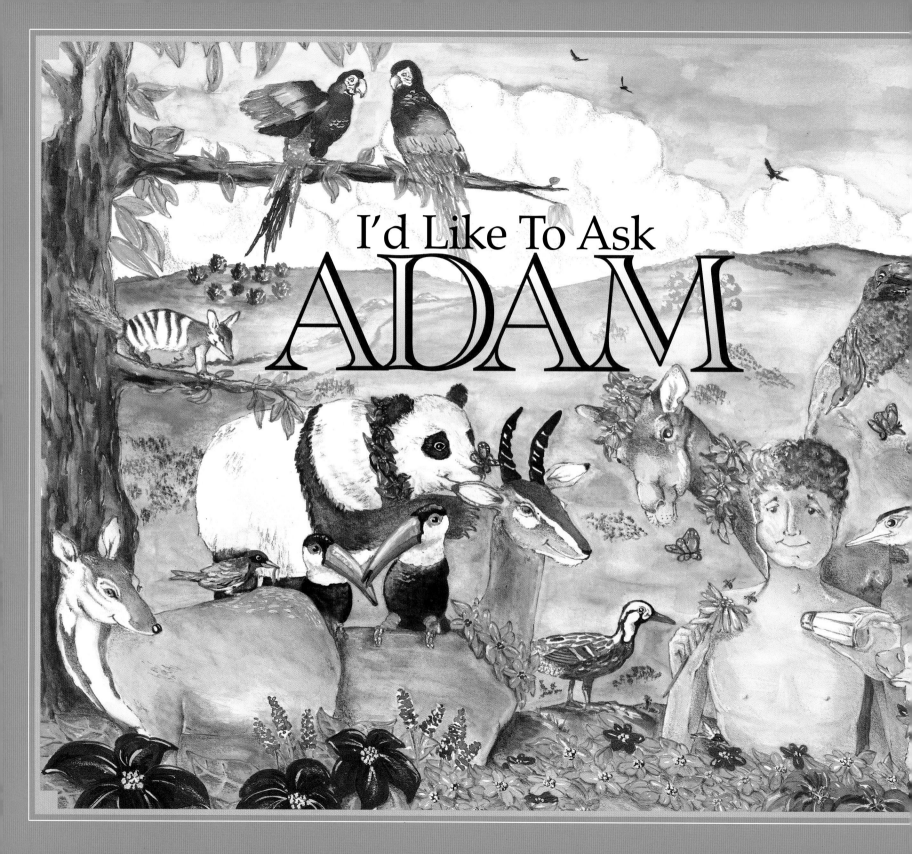

I'd Like To Ask

ADAM

NOW THE LORD GOD HAD PLANTED
A GARDEN IN THE EAST, IN EDEN;
AND THERE HE PUT THE MAN HE HAD FORMED.
GENESIS 2:8

I'd like to ask Adam . . .
When God breathed life
Into your nostrils of clay,
What did you learn
On your very first day?

Being brand new,
How did you feel?
Did you run and hop?
Did you laugh and squeal?

Did you ponder the use
Of each item God made?
Did you check out the difference
Between sunshine and shade?

Did the animals skitter
And play little games?
Were you surprised
When God brought them
To you for their names?

When you saw fluttering yellow things
Flit toward the skies,
Did you know in an instant
They'd be called butterflies?

With everything new
In the world to explore,
There was nothing you'd ever
Experienced before.

Did you touch and taste?
Did you pinch and poke?
Did your voice have a squeak
The first time you spoke?

Did you wonder why
You didn't have wings?
Did you crawl on the ground
With creeping things?

Did you look at the shape
Of each flower and bud?
Did you climb jagged rocks?
Did you slide in the mud?

Did you explore deep waters
With sharks and whales,
Or splash in ponds
With tadpoles and snails?

Did animals roam
The forest floor?
Were wild beasts tame?
Did they pace? Did they roar?

Did elephants instigate
Rollicking romps?
Did they leave an impression
With earth-shaking stomps?

When you wished for some quiet,
Did you have a discussion
About their punctuated, plopping,
Persistent percussion?

Or did they strike up their band
All calling and trumpeting,
Marching around,
Stompity stumpeting?

Now for the question
I've had on my mind:
Were you lonely without
Someone else of your kind?

Were you content to be friends
With foxes and bears
Who padded at night
To their dens and their lairs?

Did you feel lonely
Not being part of a pair?
Were you glad when God
Made a woman to care?

God caused a deep sleep,
Then took a rib from your side . . .
What an unusual way
To get a bride.

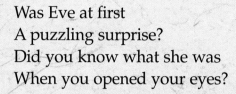

Was Eve at first
A puzzling surprise?
Did you know what she was
When you opened your eyes?

When Eve spoke
In a language you understood,
Did you whoop, did you holler,
"This is *great!* This is *good!*"

Then the Creator,
Who made you from dust,
Gave you a test
Of your love and your trust.

When God put the garden
Under your care,
Was an "Off Limits" sign
On one tree that was there?

He gave you a chance
To obey and believe,
But that leads to a question
I'd like to ask Eve.

Genesis 1–2

NOT EAT
IS FRUIT

I'd Like To Ask
EVE

Now the serpent was more crafty than any
of the wild animals the Lord God had made.
He said to the woman, "Did God really say,
'You must not eat from any tree in the garden'?"

Genesis 3:1

EAT
IT

Id like to ask Eve . . .

When you spoke with the serpent
In the garden one day,
Did you have any sense
You should be running away?

The creature, so cunning,
Tried to make God seem mean—
For not letting you eat
From one tree you had seen.

God had warned Adam
Not to eat of that tree—
Though the fruit seemed luscious,
And was pleasant to see.

Did you know if you tasted
The fruit on that day,
It would make you wise
In an unhappy way?

And something would happen
God never intended:
If you ate of the tree,
Your life would be ended.

That serpent kept twisting—
Twisting your mind,
To suggest to your head
That God was unkind.

So that really was
An obedience test;
Satan got you to doubt
God knew what was best.

Oh, but that serpent
Was wicked and wily,
He shaded the truth,
Assuring you slyly:
"If you eat of this tree—
You surely won't die!"
Did he laugh to himself
About his whopping-big lie?

Eve, did you hear
A warning deep down inside you
When you reached for the fruit
God had denied you?

You ate of the fruit
For you were deceived.
Did you find out too late
Whom you should have believed?

But you didn't fall down
In a heap right away—
You lost your life
In a spiritual way.

And so, not knowing where
This matter would end,
Did you dread to see God—
Your very best friend?

What made you know
You were naked and bare?
Who thought of stitching
Camouflage fig leaves to wear?

You tried to be invisible
Under the trees,
Hoping to hide
From the God who sees.

When God walked in the garden
In the cool of the day,
Calling, "Where are you?"
What could you say?

Trouble came
On creation that day.
Because of your deed,
You were sent away.

Did you wish to undo
The harm that you'd done?
Did you wish you'd not listened
To the slithery one?

To comfort your sorrow,
God showed mercy and love.
He promised help
Would be sent from above.

One day Satan would be crushed,
And the curse be undone.
To do this, God promised
To send His own Son.

Were you glad Jesus said
He would die in your place,
To become the Savior
For the whole human race?

One day He would rise
With new life for you,
But that isn't everything
Jesus will do.
One day He'll return
To make *everything* new.

Now, Eve, there's one more thing
I'd like to ask you:
Aren't you glad that everything
God says is true?

Genesis 2–3

I'd Like To Ask
NOAH

THE ANIMALS GOING IN WERE MALE AND FEMALE
OF EVERY LIVING THING,
AS GOD HAD COMMANDED NOAH
GENESIS 7:16

UP IF YOU WEI
UNDER 250 POU

DOWN IF YOU WE
OVER 250 POUN

 like to ask Noah...

What did you do
When you were the keeper
Of God's floating zoo?

How did you know
Each animal's name
On the day that God called them
And quickly they came—

Thumping, jumping
Leaping, creeping,
In swift obedience to
The voice of the Lord,
As they tramped up the ramp
And clattered on board?

Did the tall giraffe
Choose a special deck
To give him room,
To crane his neck?

Did the elephant have to
Stash his trunk
With his favorite things
Under his bunk?

Were the toads and lizards
And leaping things
At home in a berth
Without any springs?

And what kinds of whinings
Were needlessly said?
Did the frogs say they'd croak
With no waterbed?

And the food you amassed
Of every kind,
Was it stored fore and aft—
Up front and behind?

Did your wife and your boys
Need to give you a hand
To help you fulfill
God's weighty command?

I guess that it shouldn't
Be any surprise
That you didn't hoard water—
It came from the skies!

Did you run a pipe
From the roof to a tank
Where the creatures frolicked
And bathed and drank?

When it came time
For the critters to eat,
How did you manage
That incredible feat?

CHEESE

FOR THE BIRDS

ZEBRA CAKES

FISH NIBBLES ?

HONEY

BE ANS

NO BEARS ALLOWED

Was there lots of roaring
And clawing and neighing,
And mooing and meowing,
And barking and braying?

Or did the animals move
In orderly pairs?
Did they go below?
Or did they eat upstairs?

In the dining room
Did they take their stations
And patiently wait
For their daily rations?

When it was time
For bed at night
Did you send room service
With a final bite—
To soothe the animals
And settle them down
With a drink of water
And a warm nightgown?

Or did they sleep
In their natural coats—
The Angora cat
And the sheep and the goats?

Did the silly goose roost
And hide her head?
Or did she lie down
On her featherbed?

QUIET
PLEASE!
ANIMALS MAY
BE SLEEPING

THIS WAY

When the animals were quiet
And snuggled abed
Did they close their eyes
While your prayers were said?

Noah, did you pray
You'd peacefully sleep
While the thunder rattled
And the waters grew deep?

Did you rest—for you knew
That each creature aboard
Was made and protected
By the Almighty Lord,
Who'd gathered you into a
Waterproof farm
And was keeping you safe
From all danger and harm?

God kept the ark safe
Through each rainy, dark night.
And I know, as I'm pulling
My bedclothes up tight—
And waiting for someone
To turn out the light—
God loves me and watches
To see I'm all right.

Good night.

Genesis 6–9

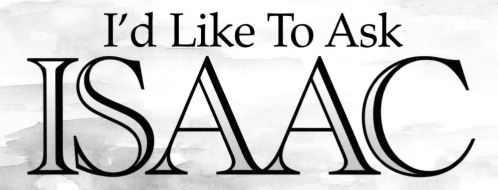

I'd Like To Ask
ISAAC

ISAAC SPOKE UP AND SAID TO HIS FATHER ABRAHAM,
"FATHER?"
"YES, MY SON?" ABRAHAM REPLIED.
"THE FIRE AND WOOD ARE HERE," ISAAC SAID,
"BUT WHERE IS THE LAMB?"
GENESIS 22:7

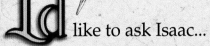

I'd like to ask Isaac...

Did your mother hug you,
As you left on your way,
For the land of Moriah
With your father one day?

She must not have known
What was coming about
When your father and you
And his servants set out.

Did you have any reason
To doubt or to fear
When your father told them,
"Hold the donkey. Stay here"?

When he added,
"We will worship and soon return"—
Did you wonder what sacrifice
Your father would burn?

As you carried a bundle
Of wood for the fire,
How long did you wait
Until you held to inquire,
"Father, where is the offering lamb
We will kill?
Is there one higher up
On the top of the hill?"

Did you know from
Learning at your father's side
That he meant every word
When he said, "God will provide"?

Isaac, were you
Confused and afraid,
When it was you who were
Bound and carefully laid
On the rough stone altar
Your father had made?

He reasoned that God
Could bring you to life
Even as he raised
The sacrifice knife.

Were you surprised
To suddenly hear
A voice speak from heaven
To your father—
Loud and clear?

"Now I know you fear God,
So don't touch the lad.
You didn't withhold
The only son that you have."

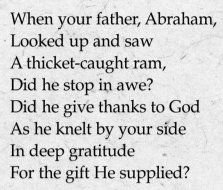

When your father, Abraham,
Looked up and saw
A thicket-caught ram,
Did he stop in awe?
Did he give thanks to God
As he knelt by your side
In deep gratitude
For the gift He supplied?

Did you see God's peace
On your father's face
When he said, *"Jehovah-Jireh,*
Is the name of this place"*?

Afterward,
For many days,
Did you wonder about
God's mysterious ways?

Did you think on
Your father's obedience—
How he trusted God
When things *didn't* make sense?

Were you sure in your heart
That God's promise was true,
That all families on earth
Would be blessed—through you?

Genesis 16–22

I'd Like To Ask
DAVID

David said to the Philistine,
"You come against me with sword and spear and
javelin, but I come against you in the name of the
Lord Almighty, the God of the armies of Israel, whom
you have defied."
1 Samuel 17:45

I'd like to ask David . . .

When you were young
And had to keep sheep,
Did you make up songs
While the sheep were asleep?

Did you play your harp
Out on the hills
To keep yourself sharp,
Practicing skills?

Did you gather smooth stones
For your leather sling?
Did you wind up and aim,
And hurl them . . . *zing?*

Could you hit a target
The breadth of a hair?
And *how* did you strike
The lion and the bear
After you grabbed them
By their bristling hair?

To rescue poor lambs
From cruel, drooling jaws,
Did you snatch little woollies
From between beastly paws?

When your father sent you to Elah
Where two armies faced off,
Your soldier brothers' greeting
Was to sneer and to scoff.

They were angry,
Saying you were
Too young and too small
To ask about fighting the giant
Who frightened them all.

When you saw Israel's brave men
Shaking with fright,
Hiding from Goliath,
Keeping out of his sight,
Did you wonder why warriors
Sheepishly ran away
When the giant roared insults at
God's army each day?

When you asked to fight
The champion,
Did the soldiers laugh—
Or cheer you on?

Would they trust themselves
To the hands of a lad?
If a shepherd boy lost . . .
Things would be bad!

They knew the rules
Of battleground duels—

If you fought and won,
Their lives would be saved.
If you lost . . . Saul's followers
Would all be enslaved.

King Saul let you fight,
And you easily won.
You became the hero
Of everyone.

This was part of God's plan
To make you a king,
But with your
Sheep-sitting background
Who'd believe such a thing—
That you'd conquer a giant
With your faith and a sling?

1 Samuel 17

I'd Like To Ask
MARY

WHEN HIS PARENTS SAW HIM, THEY WERE ASTONISHED.
HIS MOTHER SAID TO HIM,
"SON, WHY HAVE YOU TREATED US LIKE THIS?"
LUKE 2:48

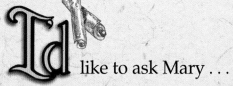 like to ask Mary . . .

When you went to the temple
For the Passover feast,
Why didn't your 12-year-old Jesus
Tell someone at least
That He was busy and
Decided to stay,
When everyone else
Was starting away?

You'd set out for home
With a very large troupe
Of animals and relatives
And friends in your group.

Only after you'd
Traveled a day,
  Descending the mountain,
  Well on your way,
 Did you feel in your bones
Something was wrong?
Jesus was not with His cousins
And friends in that throng.

And so you and Joseph
Turned around,
 You searched Jerusalem
   Up and down.

By the third frantic day,
What did you say?

Did you begin going
From door to door,
While your heart was aching
More and more—
Seeking a word or a clue
From anyone
Who might have seen
Or heard of your Son?

Did you file some sort
Of missing person's report?
What finally led you
To the temple court?

Were you tired and hungry
And a little bit scared
Till you spied Jesus talking
With teachers there?

I know your reaction.
You were astonished!
Did you and Joseph discuss
Whether Jesus should be
Hugged or admonished?

Mary, I've often wondered,
How did you say,
"Jesus, why did You
Treat us this way?"

Was that just a question
Or a very hurt cry?
And what did you think
Of Jesus' reply—
"Didn't you know I must be doing
My Father's business?"
What did He mean?
How could you guess?

Did you quietly tuck away
All these events in your heart,
Trusting God as you said,
"Come, Son, let's depart"?

Did He obey everything
You told Him to do?
The Bible says,
"He went down to Nazareth
And was obedient to you."

Luke 2

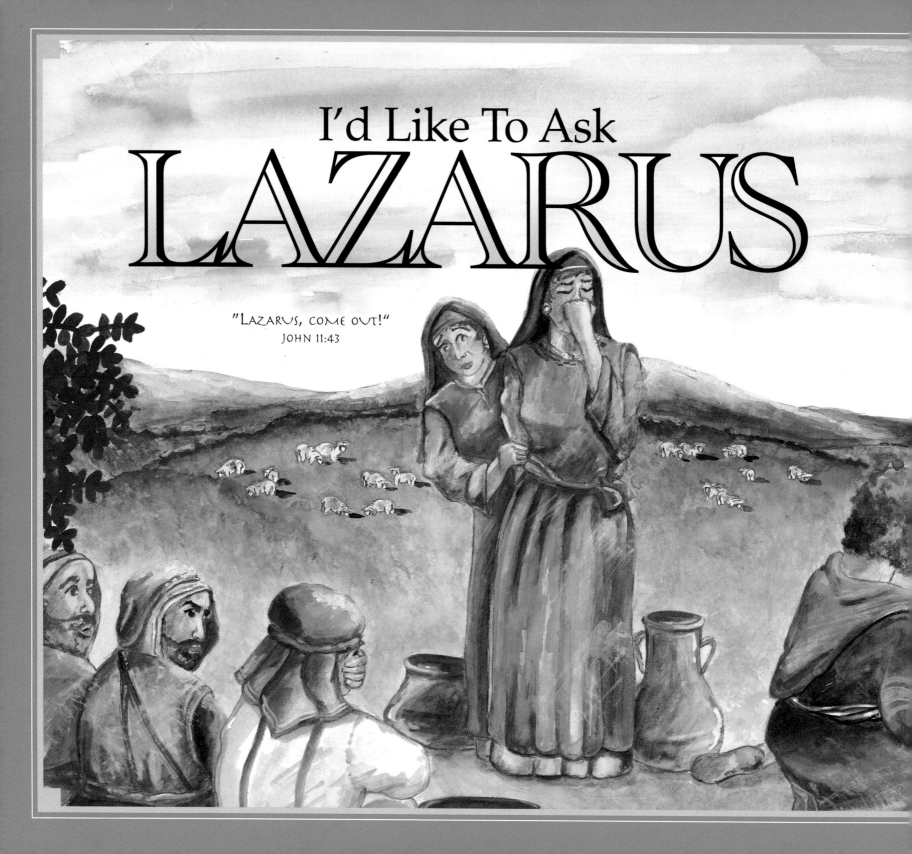

I'd like to ask Lazarus . . .

Lazarus, coming out of your tomb—
Did you step back into life
from a cavelike room?
Or did you rise
In a spectacular, supernatural *zoom*
From a rocky grave,
 At least six feet deep,
  When the Lord came to raise you,
   To wake you from sleep?

When Jesus said, "Move the stone!"
From where you'd been laid,
Were the mourners and onlookers
Upset and afraid?

Now, we know
You really were thoroughly dead
Partly from what
Martha and Mary each said,
As they trembled and sniffed
And wept, teary-eyed,
"Lord, if You'd been here
He would not have died."
Seeing their sorrow,
Jesus cried.

At the tomb, Martha blurted,
Perhaps without thinking,
"*Four days* he's been dead.
By this time he is stinking!"

Who lifted or rolled
The stone from the door?
They'd probably not helped with
A resurrection before.

For the sake of the people standing by
(Who were very sorry you had to die),
Jesus prayed to His Father
With a voice of thanksgiving
So they'd know God had sent Him
When they saw you were living.

Then when Jesus cried
With a mighty shout,
"Lazarus, come forth!"
You came out!

Jesus certainly gave you
A supernatural boost,
For you were tied
In grave clothes
And had to be loosed.

How could you walk
At any pace,
With a napkinlike blindfold
Over your face?

As you came out
And people gawked,
I wonder if *they* knew
If you flew or you walked?

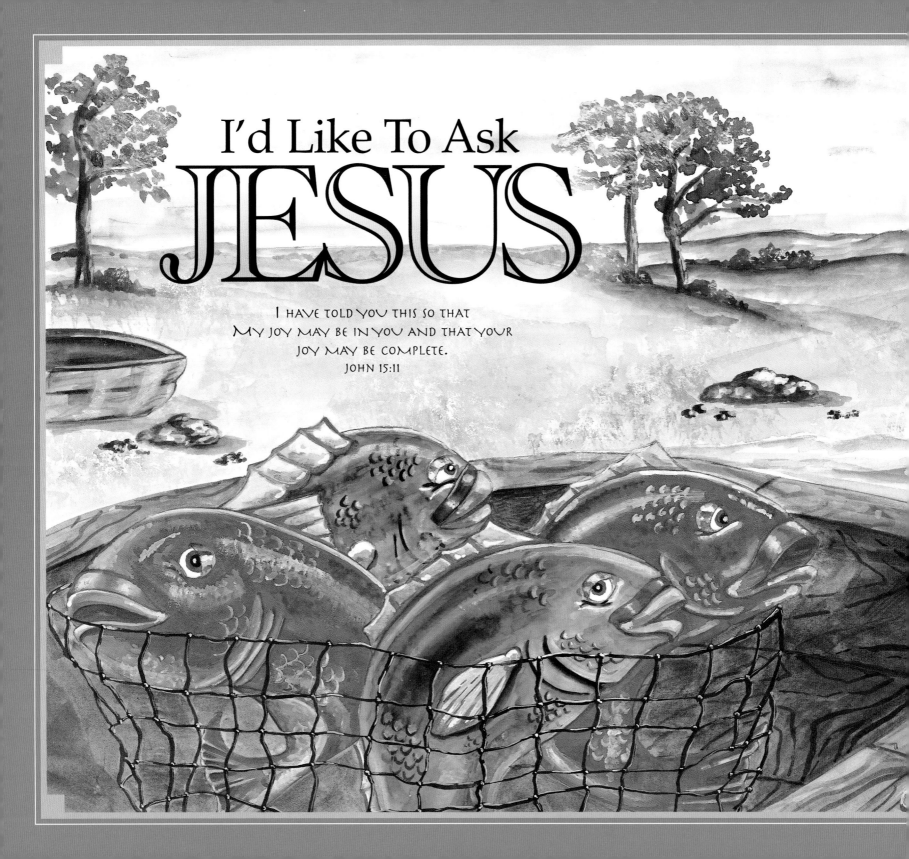

I'd like to ask Jesus . . .

I'd like to ask You
About Your friends,
And about Your joy
That never ends.

Did Your followers
Always get the gist
When Your words
Sometimes had a humorous twist?
Who understood?
Could You make a list?

You loved Mary and Martha,
Lazarus' sisters.
Did they get the points
Of Your humorous twisters?

Were Your disciples
Generally a jolly crew?
What about the fishermen
Who followed You?

When they left their nets
You gave them a line:
"You'll be fishing for men."
That wording was fine
(Perhaps a slight pun?)
To explain the new work
They'd just begun.

When crowds of thousands
Came to hear You speak,
Were Your examples sometimes
Tongue-in-cheek?

Like "swallowing a camel
After straining a gnat."
I see something
Quite funny in that.

Your words, so simple,
Are really deep
Often concerning
The rules we keep.

You ask us
In a pointed way:
"Why call me 'Lord,'
And not *do* what I say?"
It's surprising You
Love us so much, anyway.

How can it be
In creation's span,
You specifically say
Your delight is in *man?*

You came to earth
As a friend to sinners.
You are the God-Man who feasted
At weddings and dinners.

I know when You came here
You suffered and died,
So all those who love You
Could be bought as your bride.
One day we'll hear a trumpet—
And we'll fly to Your side!

At the incredible supper
We'll have with You soon,
When we're welcomed into
God's banqueting room,
Will we be laughing out loud
As stories are told?
Will we be dancing with joy
On the streets of pure gold?

Lord, I don't mean
To sound irreverent.
I trust You know
How my questions are meant.

Thank You for hearing
The things I pray.
And God, I'm waiting for
That stupendous day

When we are with You
And the Father at last.
Will our celebration
Be called a heavenly blast—
With sounding trumpets,
And angels winging,
The twenty-four elders and
God's people singing?

Will all creatures of God shout,
"Hallelujah on high"?
What a happening
You'll be hosting up there
In the sky!

It won't be a magic kingdom
That's only pretend.
We'll enjoy glory with God
That will never end.

Amen.

Matthew 5, Mark 1

GABRIEL'S "TO DO"

SEND INVITATIO
SHINE STREETS OF G
BAND PRACTIC
POLISH SILVE

A LAST WORD TO
JESUS

I asked life's most important question
When I was a kid:
I asked You to become My Savior.
I'm so glad that I did!

Thank You for hearing
Whenever we pray,
And for never turning
Our questions away.

Amen.